The Little
LOWRY

Catherine de Duve

*Explore the Life and Work
of the Much-Loved British Painter*

KATE'ART EDITIONS

AT THE TIME OF L.S. LOWRY

Laurence Stephen Lowry is born at 8 Barrett Street, Old Trafford, in Stretford, Lancashire on the 1st November 1887. He is the first and only child. Throughout his early years L.S. Lowry lives in Victoria Park, in the suburbs of Manchester.

Cotton Mills
In the nineteenth century, Manchester grew rapidly, thanks to the industrial revolution, becoming the global centre for cotton and textiles. Many textile factories appear, spinning cotton on an industrial scale, creating whole new quarters of workers' houses which can still be seen today.

Electricity
is becoming increasingly common in homes, streets, factories and railways. The world is changing! But not in every house...

Football
Manchester United Football Club is founded in 1878 and joins the football league in 1892. Manchester City Football Club is founded in 1894. Manchester United win the first FA Cup in 1904. They then move to Old Trafford. Since then they have become one of the biggest clubs in the world.

Steam Locomotives
The first railway line linking Manchester and Liverpool is built in 1830.

...MANCHESTER

In Lowry's day thousands of people work in industrial towns like Manchester. The artist paints pictures of the city around him. Lowry never travels abroad, preferring the British landscape. He likes to depict the urban industrial world. Lowry also paints portraits, seascapes, landscapes and much more…

What does Lowry paint? Look at these different paintings and drawings.

Children playing

Life in the streets

Landscape

Boy

Market places

Mills

Figures walking

Sea and yachts

Dogs

FAMILY

Lowry's father, Robert, is a clerk responsible for collecting rent. His mother, Elizabeth, is a lover of literature and wants to become a concert pianist. Unfortunately she suffers from poor health and is always irritable and nervous. She wants a delicate daughter instead of a clumsy big boy! The atmosphere at home is not an entirely happy one.

All his life Lowry has been a loner. When Lowry is little, he does not have many friends to play with, but he does have cousins. Lowry leaves school at the age of 15. His aunt said "You are no good for anything else, so you might as well go to Art School." His mother does not even like her son's pictures…

But in 1905, when Lowry is 18, he begins to take evening classes in fine art and free-hand art drawing.

 Draw like Lowry would have done in his classes.

PARK

In 1909, due to financial problems, the family move to 117 Station Road, Pendlebury, a poorer industrial part of Manchester. The house doesn't have electricity, so the young Lowry has to paint by gas light. In Pendlebury Lowry discovers a new landscape and paints textile mills and factory chimneys rather than trees.

SECRET
A naive Sunday artist? Lowry keeps his day-time job secret from the art world. He doesn't want to be treated as a part-time "Sunday painter". The truth was only made public after his death in 1976.

At 23, the young Lowry works as a rent collector for the Pall Mall Property Company in Manchester, a job he continues until his retirement in 1952, aged 65. He paints in his spare time throughout his life.

Lowry goes to the Manchester Academy of Fine Art and the Salford Royal Technical College where he develops his style. From there he has a view of Peel Park, which becomes the subject of a number of his paintings.

What does Lowry see from the window? Can you see the trees and the smoky chimneys?

FRENCH TEACHER

Adolphe Valette is born in the industrial town of St. Etienne, France, and comes to England in 1904.

At the Academy, Lowry studies under the French Impressionist *Valette*, who paints the industrial landscape. He is a pioneer of Impressionism in Manchester. Lowry's French teacher makes a big impact on him.

> I cannot over-estimate the effect on me of the coming into this drab city of Valette, full of French Impressionism, aware of everything that was going on in Paris.

Lowry studies until 1925 at the Salford Royal Technical College where he develops his style. What does he see from the window?

 Draw an industrial landscape.

INDUSTRIAL LANDSCAPE

As a modern painter, Lowry shows how the industrial revolution has transformed the towns and their surroundings. His landscapes can be seen as bleak, reflecting the painter's own state of mind.

Behind the lake the factories' chimneys spew out black smoke. Can you see the characters on the sides of the lake? What are they doing there?

Look at the painting. Find the sunken boats, the chimney fumes, the murky water and the dark gravestones.

SELF-PORTRAIT

In 1931, an exhibition of *Vincent Van Gogh*'s work is shown at Manchester Art Gallery. One year later, Lowry's father dies, leaving debts. His mother then becomes very sick and is left bed-ridden. Lowry is devoted to her. Continuing with his day-time work, he can only paint when she has fallen asleep. He paints until he can no longer keep his eyes open. How red they must be!

At this time he produces very meaningful self-portraits. Is it the influence of van Gogh's expressionism on him? "Why do you have to paint such ugly things?" asks his mother.

 Which of these is painted by Van Gogh? Which one do you prefer? Can you see the intensity in the paintings?

Vincent Van Gogh (1853-1890) is a Dutch post-Impressionist painter. His paintings are colourful and very expressive.

SECRET

Some of Lowry's paintings are painted over the surface of other images. *Head of a Man,* 1938 (the man with red eyes), when x-rayed, shows a female portrait and possibly a self-portrait underneath.

To find out more, take a look at The Little Van Gogh *in the same series.*

Do you think is a self-portrait by Lowry?

MILLS

Lowry finds new inspiration for his art in the factories and mills he sees around him every day. Are the people going to work or coming home? Here Lowry combines real buildings and structures with details from his own imagination.

I saw the industrial scene and was affected by it. Trying to draw it all the time and trying to express the industrial scene as well as possible. It wasn't easy, well, a camera could have done the scene straight off.

Which part is from Lowry's imagination? Do you hear the clop of horse hooves on cobble stones?

FIGURES

This picture returns to one of his favourite themes: a mass of workers coming to and from the factory, all the time watched by the smoking chimneys towering above them.

Are all the houses identical?

🔍 Look at the long figures. Compare the two paintings. Which is coming home from work and which is going to the factory?

DRAWINGS

Lowry always goes around with a pencil and piece of paper or a sketch book in his pocket. He often makes quick sketches on the spot. Back home, he composes his work and carefully places each figure.

🔍 Look at the two churches.
What difference do you see?
Which technique do you prefer?

Drawing

Oil

OIL

Lowry uses a very basic range of colours, which he mixes on his palette and paints on a white background to create an industrial sky.

I like oils... you can work into them over a period of time.

SECRET
Did Lowry wear an apron? Someone once asked, "What do you do with your old suits?", "Wear them", came the reply! Lowry certainly wears them for work, wiping the brushes on his lapels and sleeves.

As Lowry, choose your favourite colours to paint this canvas.

THE FIGHT!

What's happening? A fight! Why are they fighting? They are outside a lodging house in Manchester. In the window of the building is the price of a bed and breakfast for the night.

Look at the scene. Write down what you think the witnesses are saying about the fight.

LONELINESS

If it were not for loneliness, none of my works would have happened. Sadness attracts me, and there are some very sad things. I find similar feelings in myself.

Lowry also paints loneliness and sadness by painting deserted scenes. The silence of the hills is shown by the empty darkness of the scene. The lake reflects the vast white sky. Where are we? Is it a real landscape or a dream? Do you see anybody?

Look closely at this picture. What do you feel? Imagine a story that could take place in this picture.

WHITE SKY

Lowry's skies are mainly white. Lowry wants to find beautiful shades of white in his work. He loves seeing the sky become blurred and creamy as it meets the land. His white background becomes a creamy grey-white.

It's your turn! Carry on this painting in the style of Lowry. Make it mysterious!

MARKET

This is Pendlebury Market, close to Lowry's home. Sometimes, as well as deserted landscapes, Lowry paints the crowded but lonely life in the city, including factories, markets, busy streets and schools.

All my people are lonely. Crowds are the most lonely thing of all.

 Find the pram and the loneliest people in this painting. How many dogs do you see?

18

FIRST EXHIBITIONS

1939, the year that Lowry creates this painting, is also the year that sees his first London exhibition. After the war, he again exhibits in London and sells 20 paintings!

Which of these details are not the same as in the painting?

What is the child holding?

What's in the basket?

What time is it?

WAR

Lowry's mother dies in October 1939 and Lowry falls into depression, neglecting the upkeep of his house. The Second World War is declared. During the war he serves as a volunteer fire watcher and becomes an official war artist in 1943. He draws the ruins of bombed buildings.

 Find all of these features in the painting below.

LOWRY'S HOUSE

In 1948 Lowry buys a modest house called "The Elms" in Mottram-in-Longdendale. He thinks this house is ugly and uncomfortable, but stays there for the rest of his life. The dining room there becomes his studio, his "workroom".

Lowry drew different houses. Which would you choose to live in?

LEVEL CROSSING

 Attention! The steam train is passing at the level crossing. The red flag indicates that pedestrians cannot pass. His characters are painted in Lowry's unique style. Dogs look on in wonder at the large machine.

 Who are these characters? What are they doing?

REVELATION

One day Lowry misses his train. He is cross. When he goes back up the steps, he sees a mill. It is a great red square block inbetween a bunch of little terraced houses. Lowry has a revelation. "Suddenly, I knew what I had to paint."

Imagine what Lowry sees when he leaves the train station. Draw it below.

SEASCAPE

All his life Lowry has been drawn to the sea. He starts going to the seaside as a boy. He goes to North Wales and the Fylde Coast with his parents. Later he takes some annual holidays to the seaside, first in Berwick-upon-Tweed, in the North East of England. Later in 1960, the painter regularly visits Sunderland, County Durham. He likes to look out at the North Sea, sometimes quiet, sometimes crowded with ships.

> I have been fond of the sea all my life. How wonderful yet terrible it is.

Simple lines of thick colour depict the seascape. What colours does he use for the sea, the sky and the beach? Is it sunny, rainy or cloudy?

YACHTS

The artist is captivated by the seaside and paints scenes of the beaches, docksides and yachts. He walks beside the sea for hours.

When he has no sketchbook, Lowry draws on the back of envelopes, serviettes and cloakroom tickets.

Like Lowry, draw a sketch on the back of this envelope.

WHO'S THAT GIRL?

Lowry is a solitary man. He never marries. He is shy and a bit eccentric. He likes to tell stories to his friends. The painter has a great sense of humour, however. He likes to make jokes. In his living room he has a collection of clocks from his mother. "What time is it?" he asks his friends. He has set all the clocks to different times!

Who's that girl? It looks like a formal portrait. Lowry keeps this picture in his house.

SECRET
Throughout his career, Lowry paints stylised portraits of a mysterious girl called "Ann". She appears in many of his paintings and sketches. But still no-one knows who this lady is.

PORTRAIT

Imagine a portrait of a mysterious person.
Choose the colour of the eyes, the hair, the skin, the mouth and the clothes.

BIG FEET

For forty years, L.S. Lowry walks all over the city for his job collecting rent, witnessing scenes that inspire him. He discovers narrow cobbled streets and meets all types of people to collect money from. He sees his subjects all around him!

 Who are these characters? They have long arms and big feet...Draw a tall figure with clown feet.

CHILDREN

Lowry often asks children what they think of his paintings. "Because they tell the truth" says Lowry. The artist paints the children that he sees in the street. What are they doing? What are they thinking?

✏️ Write down what you think about Lowry's art.

_____
_____
_____
_____
_____
_____
_____
_____

FAMOUS!

Lowry becomes famous when he is older . "It has all come too late". As he said "I am a simple man". Lowry declines many honours, including a knighthood. "I have been thanked enough… People have liked my pictures."

In 1967 the Post Office issue a stamp featuring one of his paintings.

 Be a famous artist and create your own stamp.

A SIMPLE MAN

L. S. Lowry dies of pneumonia in hospital on the 23rd February 1976, aged 88. He is buried in the Southern Cemetery in Manchester. He left around 1,000 paintings and over 8,000 drawings.

Text and illustrations : Catherine de Duve
Concept and production: Kate'Art Editions
Proofreading: Stuart Forward

L.S. Lowry: Coming from the Mill, 1930: cover, p.2, 3 (detail), p.10 | Group of People, 1959: cover (details), p.28 | The Cripples, 1949: p.29 (details) | Self-Portrait, 1925: p.1, p.2 | Level Crossing, 1946: p.2 (detail), p.3 (detail), p.22 | Boy in a School Cap, 1912: p.3 (detail) | Market Scene, Northern Town, 1939: cover (detail), p.3 (detail), p.6 (detail), p.16 (detail), p.18, p.19, p. 30 (detail) | Behind Leaf Square, 1926: p.3 (detail) | The Lake, 1937: p.3 (detail), p.7 | Head from the Antique, c1908: p.4| Nude Boy Seated, 1906: p.4 | Band Stand, Peel Park, Salford, 1925: p.5 | View from the Window of the Royal Technical College, looking towards Broughton, 1925: p.6 | Head of a Man (With Red Eyes), 1938: p.9 | Blitzed Site, 1942: p.20 | Gentleman Looking at Something, 1960: p.10, 24, 28 (detail) | Going to Work, 1959: p.3 (detail), p.11 | A Street Scene (St Simon's Church), 1927: p.12 | A Street Scene (St Simon's Church), 1928: p.2 (detail), p.3 (detail), p.12 | A Fight, c1935: p.14 | Two People, 1962: p.15|Landscape in Cumberland, 1951: p.16 (detail) | A Landmark, 1936: p.16 | The Lake, 1951: p.16 (detail), p.17 (detail) | House on the Moor, 1950: p.21 (detail) | The Steps, Peel Park, Salford, 1930: p. 21 (detail) | Oldfield Road Dwellings, 1929: p. 21 (detail) | Houses in Broughton (Back: Street Scene 1924), 1937: p.21 (detail) | North James Henry Street, Salford, 1956: p.21 (detail) | An Old Farm, 1943: p.21 (detail) | Seascape, 1952: p.24 | Yachts, 1959: p.3 (detail), p.25 | Portrait of Ann, 1957: p.26 | Going to the Match, 1953: p.2 (detail), p.28 | Man Lying on a Wall, 1957: p.30

Photography: L.S. Lowry: p.12, p.13, p.31
© The Lowry Collection, Salford.

Adolphe Valette: *Self-portrait*, c1912: p.7
Vincent Van Gogh: Paris: Orsay Museum: *Self Portrait*, 1889: p.8

With thanks to:
The Lowry, Salford Quays, Stuart Foward, Véronique Lux, Chantal Guyot, Eric Vaes and all those who assisted in making this book.

Our books are available in various languages:
English, French, German, Dutch, Italian, Spanish, Japanese, Danish and Russian.

Go to www.kateart.com
and visit our online shop

info@kateart.com